MEMPHIS

The Delaplaine
2022
Long Weekend Guide

No business listed in this guide has provided *anything* free to be included.

Andrew Delaplaine

Senior Writer - **James Cubbv**

MEMPHIS
The Delaplaine
Long Weekend Guide

TABLE OF CONTENTS

Chapter 1
WHY MEMPHIS?

Though Memphis is the biggest city in Tennessee, Nashville is the capital. There's always been something of a rivalry between the two cities.

Nashville may claim to be "Music Capital of the World," but Memphis is almost universally recognized as the home of the Blues.

And Elvis? Where did the King choose to live? Memphis has **Graceland**, Elvis Presley's big mansion that draws tens of thousands of visitors a year.

Like many another city I've covered, Memphis has rediscovered its Downtown area after leaving it to rot for decades. New businesses are thriving, artists are creating exciting storefronts and galleries, the retail scene is getting more interesting, new bars are popping up.

The Orpheum

Woodruff Fontaine House

Memphis also is developing as a center for innovative cuisine, not as advanced as Nashville is (yet), but things are happening.

One thing you can do in Memphis just about cheaper than you can anywhere else is eat some of the best BBQ to be found in America. There are countless places serving up Memphis style BBQ. (Actually, I did count once, and there are about 75 BBQ places in the area.) There are dozens of places where it's hard to spend more than $10 for a meal consisting of a pulled pork sandwich, a side of fries and a soft drink or iced tea. I haven't seen this miracle anywhere else. I mean, I can show you how to eat cheap even in New York, but unless you're in Queens, where there are hundreds of fine ethnic eateries, you have to seek the best places.

Payne's

As I wrote after visiting **Payne's Original Bar-B-Que** in the listings below, when you say BBQ in Memphis, you mean pork shoulder, not ribs so much. Every little joint has its own "secret" method of handling the fire and wood.

The pork is always slow-roasted and then "pulled" by hand from the bone or chopped with the kind of cleavers you see in horror movies. The resultant pile of savory meat is placed on any of dozens of types of hamburger style buns and then topped with a dollop of coleslaw. Sauce is either added or it's not, depending on the place you're visiting. I have often spent my entire trip in Memphis eating nothing but BBQ.

And not regretted it one minute.

My last word of advice: you won't either.

HOTEL

Chapter 2
WHERE TO STAY

BIG CYPRESS LODGE AT THE PYRAMID
1 Bass Pro Dr, Memphis, 1-800-223-3333
www.big-cypress.com
NEIGHBORHOOD: Uptown
Nestled among large indoor cypress trees with a strong focus on the Bass Pro Shops outdoor lifestyle, this is one of the most unique hotels in Memphis. Set in a pyramid-shaped building boasting a wilderness-themed retail space and entertainment venues, this rustic-chic 104 guestroom hotel features rooms with a hunting lodge-inspired décor. Amenities: Complimentary Wi-Fi, flat-screen TVs, and mini-fridges. Hotel features; 2 restaurants, an aquarium, an ocean-themed bowling alley, fitness room, a day spa,

and a 25-story free-standing elevator ride.
Conveniently located 1.7 miles from Beale Street and
the National Civil Rights Museum.

GUEST HOUSE AT GRACELAND
3600 Elvis Presley Blvd, Memphis, 901-443-3000
www.guesthousegraceland.com
NEIGHBORHOOD: Whitehaven
Located in the center of a Graceland-inspired
complex, this 20-suite Guest House welcomes guests
with Southern hospitality and a royal treatment
befitting "the King." (It's really just a big boring
modern hotel, and while it is quite charmless, it does
have all the basics, if that's what you'll settle for.)
Amenities: Flat screen TVs, complimentary Wi-Fi,
Bluetooth media hubs, and coffee machines.
Facilities: Outdoor pool, entertainment facilities,
Lobby Bar, and EP's Bar & Grill. Just a 4-minute

walk from Graceland and 8 miles from the Beale
Street Historic District. Pets weighing less than 35
pounds are allowed in some rooms (daily fee).

HU. HOTEL
79 Madison Ave, Memphis, 833-585-0030
https://huhotelmemphis.com/
NEIGHBORHOOD: Downtown
Located in a downtown high-rise, this four-diamond
hotel offers 110 guest rooms, many with river views.
The fairly new hotel luxury boutique hotel boasts a
cool urban design with modern furnishings and
upscale lodgings. Working through the Memphis
Artists Spotlight program, they display the work of
local artists in the public rooms. This building used to
be a bank. The gym in the basement is in the 100-
year-old vault. Amenities include: 24-hour room
service, wireless high-speed internet access, valet
laundry, private wine reserves, spa inspired rain
showers, 37" flat screen LCD TVs, and Keurig coffee
makers. On-site dining available at an upscale eatery

with a globally inspired menu. The hotel's rooftop bar
serves handcrafted cocktails and light bites, not to
mention superior views of the Mighty Mississippi.
On-site 30-foot lap pool.

JAMES LEE HOUSE
690 Adams Ave, Memphis, 901-359-6750
www.jamesleehouse.com
NEIGHBORHOOD: Victorian Village
This historic bed and breakfast (built in 1848 and
once an arts conservatory) offers guests luxurious and
comfortable accommodations. This beats the hell out
of the run-of-the-mill lodging selection one finds here
in Memphis, for the most part. This opulent home
features five beautifully appointed suites. You won't
believe when you walk into this place that it was only
restored in 2014, and many Victorian highlights were
brought back to life: the frescoed ceiling, elaborate
golden Victorian cornices and mirrors, the intricate
moldings, distressed fireplaces. But thoroughly
modern touches are welcome, like the TempurPedic

mattresses and rain showers. Amenities include: free gourmet breakfast with made-to-order eggs, gated private parking, large LED cable TVs, and free wireless Internet access.

PEABODY HOTEL
149 Union Ave, Memphis, 901-529-4000
www.peabodymemphis.com
This luxury hotel is known for the "Peabody Ducks" that make daily treks to the lobby from the rooftop. Here guests experience the historic opulence and Southern hospitality befitting a four-Diamond hotel in its 464 smoke-free deluxe guest rooms, including 15 luxurious suites. (I usually stay here when I come to town, if I'm not trying out a B&B.) Amenities include: Pet-friendly rooms available, heated indoor pool and day spa, athletic club, in-room dining, complete audiovisual services, free newspaper, 42" flat screen TV with premium cable stations and on-command movies, and high-speed wireless internet access. On-site dining available at Peabody's award-

winning restaurants, bars, and eateries. (See the listings for **CHEZ PHILIPPE** in Restaurant section.) The Peabody offers a variety of boutiques including The Lucky Duck that specializes in duck-themed items.

THE TALBOT HEIRS

99 South Second St, 800-955-3956 or 901-527-9772
www.talbotheirs.com
NEIGHBORHOOD: Downtown
Located in the heart of downtown Memphis, this unique guesthouse features 7 spacious suites, each totally different, with kitchens. (You'll have to use the stairs.) I love this place when I'm here for extended periods. Amenities include: CD player, cable TV with HBO and other movie channels, coffee maker, and free high-speed internet access. Snacks, juice, milk, coffee, and tea are provided each day. Exercise equipment (stationary bike, stepper, and

treadmill) available for use within your suite. Conveniently located near local attractions, museums, restaurants, and nightlife.

15

Chapter 3
WHERE TO EAT

A & R BAR-B-QUE
NEIGHBORHOOD: East Memphis
3721 Hickory Hill Rd, Memphis, 901-365-9777
NEIGHBORHOOD: Whitehaven
1802 Elvis Presley Blvd, Memphis, 901-774-7444
www.aandrbbq.com
CUISINE: Barbeque
DRINKS: No Booze
SERVING: Lunch & Dinner daily
PRICE RANGE: $
Even though I rhapsodize about the "pulled" or "chopped" pork shoulder sandwiches that make Memphis BBQ so unique in other restaurants, here I always go for the Memphis style ribs. They are just

out of this world. Hold up a rib and give it a little shake and the meat will fall off. It's that tender and juicy. Be sure you order the dry version (no sauce) so you can fully absorb the complex flavors that went into this dish. (You can add sauce later.)

ALCENIA'S
317 N Main St, 901-523-0200
www.alcenias.com
CUISINE: Soul Food, Desserts
DRINKS: No Booze
SERVING: 9 – 5 Tuesday-Saturday; closed Sunday & Monday; late breakfast or lunch
PRICE RANGE: $
NEIGHBORHOOD: Uptown
Owner Alcenia's daughter often welcomes guests with a hug, making it a popular place among locals. The menu features home-style soul food. Menu favorites include: Salmon croquettes, Chicken and waffles, and if you want fried chicken, skip it and get the baked chicken; the bread pudding, the custard pie and the sweet potato pie are the standouts on the

dessert menu. Also, when was the last time you
walked into a restaurant where the owner hugged
you?

ARCADE RESTAURANT
540 South Main St, 901-526-5757
www.arcaderestaurant.com
CUISINE: Southern Diner
DRINKS: No Booze
SERVING: Breakfast & Lunch (7 to 3 daily)
PRICE RANGE: $
NEIGHBORHOOD: Downtown
Located in the center of the historic district, this
restaurant (it's really a diner, not so much a
"restaurant") takes you back in time. It's got booths
upholstered in squeaky plastic against the windows
and those uncomfortable bar stools at the counter that
are riveted to the floor so you can't move them. But
as painful as they are on my big butt, I always sit at
the counter when I can so you can talk to the

waitresses, which is half the fun. Several films were shot here: "Great Balls of Fire," "The Client," "The Firm," "Walk the Line" and "21 Grams," among them. Avoid the weekends for breakfast if you can, as it gets pretty crowded. The Southern breakfasts are a big hit here (think sweet potato pancakes with eggs and grits). Menu favorites include: Chicken and Dumplings and Chicken Spaghetti. A wide range of sandwiches, salads and pizzas for lunch. Or get what was said to be Elvis's favorite sandwich: fried peanut butter & banana. (Makes me want to puke.)

ALCHEMY BAR
940 South Cooper St, Memphis, 901-726-4444
www.alchemymemphis.com
CUISINE: Tapas
DRINKS: Full Bar
SERVING: Dinner nightly and Lunch only on Sunday
PRICE RANGE: $$$
NEIGHBORHOOD: Cooper-Young
A casual hipster eatery featuring a simple menu of Tapas and New American cuisine. Menu favorites include: Chili Roasted Fish Tacos and Coriander Crusted Lamb Chop. Great choice for brunch. Gluten-free options available.

ANDREW MICHAEL ITALIAN KITCHEN
712 W Brookhaven Cir, Memphis, 901-347-3569
www.andrewmichaelitaliankitchen.com
CUISINE: Italian
DRINKS: Full Bar
SERVING: Dinner; closed Sun & Mon

PRICE RANGE: $$$
This Beard Award Semi-Finalist is touted as
Memphis' most celebrated restaurant. Menu features
many Italian favorites and specialties like Duck with
root vegetables. Great dessert choices like the Maple
Tart. Menu changes daily.

THE BAR-B-Q SHOP
1782 Madison Ave, Memphis, 901-272-1277
www.dancingpigs.com
CUISINE: Barbeque
DRINKS: Beer & Wine Only
SERVING: Lunch & Dinner
PRICE RANGE: $$
NEIGHBORHOOD: Midtown
This place is home to the famous **Dancing Pigs BBQ**
sauce and seasoning and it's known as "Best in
Memphis." If you're into spicy BBQ, then this is your
place. (It's done in a Buffalo style.) The menu offers

items like spicy ribs and pulled pork sandwich. (They use Texas toast instead of a bun, which is nice.) If you like the sauce, they sell it to go.

BAR DKDC
964 South Cooper St, Memphis, 901-272-0830
www.bardkdc.com
CUISINE: Tapas
DRINKS: Full Bar
SERVING: Dinner; closed Sun & Mon
PRICE RANGE: $$
NEIGHBORHOOD: Cooper-Young
This bar offers Chef Karen Carrier's eclectic menu of local cuisines and international street food. Nice cocktails. Menu changes often. Live music on the weekends.

THE BEAUTY SHOP RESTAURANT
966 Cooper St, Memphis, 901-272-7111
www.thebeautyshoprestaurant.com
CUISINE: Caribbean/American
DRINKS: Full Bar
SERVING: Lunch & Dinner
PRICE RANGE: $$
NEIGHBORHOOD: Cooper-Young
Located in a former '60s beauty parlor, this kitschy New American eatery offers a menu as fun as the décor. Dinner favorites include: Grilled Espresso Honey Lamb Loin Chops and Sugar & Spiced Peking Duck. Great choice for Sunday Brunch.

BRAD'S BAR-B-Q

2845 Bartlett Rd, Bartlett, Tenn., 901-373-6326
www.bradsbarbq.com
CUISINE: Barbeque
DRINKS: No Booze
SERVING: Lunch & Dinner
PRICE RANGE: $$
NEIGHBORHOOD: Bartlett
Just across the Tennessee border (but only about 20 minutes from Downtown Memphis) you'll find the infamous Memphis-style dry rub BBQ that keeps people coming back for more. Everything seems to come with sides like juicy baked beans, spicy may saw, potato spears and greasy onion rings. No booze here but delicious sweet iced tea.

BROTHER JUNIPER'S

3519 Walker Ave, Memphis, 901-324-0144
www.brotherjunipers.com

CUISINE: BreakfastAmerican
DRINKS: No Booze
SERVING: Breakfast & Lunch
PRICE RANGE: $$
This is a total old school diner that serves only breakfast and lunch. Typical diner fare. Their fried chicken recipe is carefully guarded.

CATHERINE & MARY'S
272 S Main St, Memphis, 901-254-8600
www.catherineandmarys.com

CUISINE: Italian / Modern European
DRINKS: Full Bar
SERVING: Dinner, Lunch/Brunch only on Sundays
PRICE RANGE: $$$
NEIGHBORHOOD: Downtown

Industrial-chic eatery (situated in the historic **Hotel Chisca**) featuring Tuscan & Sicilian cuisine adapted with Memphis twists. It's supposed to evoke the memory you grandmother's cooking, assuming, of course, that your grandma came from either Tuscany or Sicily, which is quite a stretch. Combine all these "influences" and you have, well… whatever it is, it's GREAT. Couldn't be a better choice if you have only one night in Memphis. Award-winning team turns everything they touch to gold. Menu changes every month, shifting to reflect what's freshest in produce. Lots of the meats come from the chefs' own butchery. This is one of the few Memphis spots that has an in-house pastry chef, so the desserts deserve a second (or even a third) look, because you'll want to sample a couple of them, so save room. (I had the Torta del Nona (chocolate, hazelnut, Benne seed brittle, pomegranate & cream—out of this world). There's also a happy hour starting at 4, so take advantage of it if you only have a little time and can't make dinner. Favorites: Francobelli Pasta and Beef Lasagna. Main dishes and small plates to share. Nice wine & cocktails selection.

Afternoon Tea at The Peabody

CHEZ PHILIPPE
The Peabody Hotel
149 Union Ave, Memphis, 901-529-4188

<u>www.peabodymemphis.com</u>
CUISINE: French / Afternoon Tea
DRINKS: Full Bar
SERVING: Lunch & Dinner; Closed 3 days (Sun – Tues)
PRICE RANGE: $$$$
NEIGHBORHOOD: Downtown

This is the Peabody hotel's opulent main dining room offering pre-fix menu selections of 4 or 7 course dinners. (The Peabody is famous for its duck parade every morning—a "duckmaster" leads a gaggle of ducks through the lobby and to steps that lead up to a fountain in the lobby where they spend the rest of the day.) Anyway, the dining room is perfect for a dressy night out. (In fact, they would like it if gents wore jackets.) It's nice that they still prepare Caesar salad tableside. Very few places do that anymore. Favorites: Filet Mignon and the Dessert Soufflé. Nice wine pairings. Feeling a yen for afternoon tea? This is the only place I know in Memphis that serves it in high style. By the way, there's a lot more going on at The Peabody than Chez Philippe. There's a great **Lobby Bar at the Peabody**, a well-attended spot for a drink after work, **Peabody Corner Bar** (with a nice selectin of bar grub), the **Peabody Deli & Desserts** shop, great for coffee and a sweet pastry in the morning, and the **Capriccio Grill**, a superb chophouse featuring excellent steaks on a menu that slants heavily toward the Italian. Of course, if you're lodging at The Peabody (which I usually do when I'm in town), you know and appreciate all this.

CORKY'S RIBS & BBQ

5259 Poplar Ave, Memphis, 901-685-9744
www.corkysmemphis.com
CUISINE: Barbeque
DRINKS: Full Bar
SERVING: Lunch & Dinner
PRICE RANGE: $$
NEIGHBORHOOD: Eastgate
Here the BBQ meats are slow cooked over hickory wood and charcoal. This place is more "commercial" than a lot of the other joints in town. Slicker. Try the hand pulled pork sandwich served hot with cole slaw – it might be the best deal in Memphis.

CENTRAL BBQ

NEIGHBORHOOD: Midtown
2249 Central Ave, Memphis, 901-272-9377
NEIGHBORHOOD: Downtown
147 E Butler, Memphis, 901-672-7760
NEIGHBORHOOD: East
4375 Summer, Memphis, 901-767-4672
www.cbqmemphis.com
CUISINE: Barbeque
DRINKS: Beer & Wine Only
SERVING: Lunch & Dinner
PRICE RANGE: $$

Central has taken top honors in the ever-ongoing "Best BBQ in Memphis" sweepstakes about a dozen times. What do they do? They "slow smoke" all their meats: ribs, pork, chicken, turkey, beef brisket, sausage and bologna. Their premium meats are rubbed with a secret combination of dry spices, marinated for 24 hours, then smoked low and slow in the pit over a combination of hickory and pecan woods. No sauce is ever introduced into the pit.

(Whatever you order, start with their smoked hot chicken wings.) The meat here is piled higher than in most other BBQ joints. If you opt for the pork plate, see if they can give you "extra bark." That's the extra thick crust on the meat that brings with it a heavy smokiness you'll love. You'll also like the young, lively crowd that comes here from the nearby colleges. Take home an order of their homemade potato chips. They are specially cut thick and they are "salted" with a house blend that's completely unique and mouthwatering.

CHARLIE VERGOS' RENDEZVOUS

52 S 2nd St, Memphis, 901-523-2746
www.hogsfly.com
CUISINE: Barbeque
DRINKS: Beer & Wine Only
SERVING: 4:30 to 10:30 Tuesday-Thursday; 11 to 11 Friday & Saturday; closed Sunday & Monday
PRICE RANGE: $$
NEIGHBORHOOD: Downtown
Here the ribs are not wet and they're not dry. Charlie Vergos opened this place in 1948. He was Greek, and as part of his special recipe, just before they serve the ribs, they baste them in a vinegar-based marinade and then sprinkle a blend of spices over the meat. Charlie died in 2010, but he left the place to his kids who make the ribs the same way Charlie did. There's nothing quite like in anywhere in town. This place is in a basement down an alleyway in Downtown, but once you go in, you'll see how big it is. And the "rendezvous" is not just a tagline. Everybody comes here eventually, whether you're the president or a

Rolling Stone. Lots of interesting memorabilia on the walls, too. (They've developed a huge mail-order business and deliver their BBQ to you by Fedex.)

COZY CORNER
735 N Parkway, Memphis, 901-527-9158
www.cozycornerbbq.com
CUISINE: Barbeque
DRINKS: Beer & Wine Only
SERVING: 11 to 9 Tuesday-Saturday
PRICE RANGE: $$
NEIGHBORHOOD: Midtown
The BBQ is authentic at this little storefront shop with a self-service counter and a small dining room. What's really special here (and you won't find this anywhere else in Memphis but here) is the whole Cornish hen that is BBQ-ed to perfection. So moist and flavorful. The rib tips are the other thing I like

here after the Cornish hen. The spare-ribs are roasted over charcoal until tender but some folks say the best dish in the house is the barbecued baloney. (Not me. I think it's disgusting.)

ELWOOD'S SHACK

4523 Summer Ave, Memphis, 901-761-9898
www.Elwoodsshack.com
CUISINE: American (Traditional) / BBQ
DRINKS: No Booze
SERVING: Breakfast, Lunch, & Dinner
PRICE RANGE: $
NEIGHBORHOOD: Berclair

And "shack" it is. You can't get more down home than this no-frills BBQ eatery offering a menu of comfort food including smoked meats, burgers, tacos, hot dogs & sandwiches. A few picnic tables outside. Inside, they've thrown up a bunch of college teams pennants in a half-hearted attempt to create a little atmosphere, but it doesn't really matter. Ultra-cheap breakfast, and it's really good. Favorites: Brisket Taco and the juicy Hot Dogs. Daily specials deserve a second look.

ERLING JENSEN – THE RESTAURANT
1044 S Yates Rd, Memphis, 901-763-3700
www.ejensen.com
CUISINE: French / American (New)
DRINKS: Full Bar
SERVING: Dinner
PRICE RANGE: $$$$
NEIGHBORHOOD: Eastgate
In this small contemporary restaurant, you'll find Erling serving French-inspired classic seafood & beef dishes in an intimate setting. Favorites: Crab tortellini and Wagyu beef. Menu features unusual dishes like Antelope and Elk Chops. Impressive wine list and amazing cocktails. Reservations recommended.

FLIGHT

39 S Main St, Memphis, 901-521-8005
www.flightmemphis.com
CUISINE: American (New)
DRINKS: Full Bar
SERVING: Dinner, Lunch & Dinner on Sundays
PRICE RANGE: $$$
NEIGHBORHOOD: Downtown

A classy Gordon Ramsay restaurant with a wine flight theme. There's a nice outdoor area on Main Street. Inside, there's a 2-level dining room elegantly laid out. You can sample small portions of multiple main courses, all with a variety of paired wines and appetizers. Favorites: Duck Confit and Steak & Lobster. Delicious bread pudding dessert.

FOLK'S FOLLY
551 S Mendenhall Rd, Memphis, 901-762-8200
www.folksfolly.com
CUISINE: Steakhouse
DRINKS: Full Bar
SERVING: Dinner
PRICE RANGE: $$$
NEIGHBORHOOD: Brennan
Upscale steakhouse offering prime cut meats and seafood in a white tablecloth setting with excellent service and a clubby atmosphere. Weekly specials. Favorites: Veal Piccata and Smoked Pork Chop.

Piano bar in Cellar Lounge. Retail shop offers take-home orders and gift packages.

THE FOUR WAY
998 Mississippi Blvd, 901-507-1519
www.fourwaymemphis.com
CUISINE: Soul Food, Southern
DRINKS: No Booze
SERVING: Lunch & Dinner (11 till 7 p.m., but only
5 p.m. Saturday); closed Monday
PRICE RANGE: $
NEIGHBORHOOD: Southside
This historic soul food restaurant (since 1946) serves
great Southern dishes like fried catfish and turkey and
dressing. Menu favorites include: Salmon Croquet;
Liver & Onions; and Country Fried Steak. The sides
are great: smothered cabbage (I could make a meal of
this alone); turnip greens; fried green tomatoes;

boiled okra; broccoli & cheese. Peach cobbler for
dessert unless you go for the lemon meringue pie.

GIBSON DONUTS
760 Mt Moriah Rd, Memphis, 901-682-8200
CUISINE: Donuts & Bagels
DRINKS: No Booze
SERVING: 24 Hours
PRICE RANGE: $
NEIGHBORHOOD: Midtown
This donut shop, making donuts since 1967, offers a
larger variety than most. There's plenty of seating so
you can grab a donut or bagel with some coffee and
chill. The varieties of donuts here is amazing
including: chocolate filled, apple pie, red velvet, and
maple bacon.

GRAY CANARY
301 S Front St, Memphis, 901-249-2932
www.thegraycanary.com

CUISINE: Seafood
DRINKS: Full Bar
SERVING: Dinner; Closed Mondays
PRICE RANGE: $$$-$$$$
NEIGHBORHOOD: Downtown
So precise it almost looks stage-managed is this
"Industrial chic" seafood eatery overlooking the
water. As sleek as it is, they aren't trying to cover for
poor quality food—everything here is superlative.
Favorites: Murder Point Oysters and Lamb. Raw bar
usually has 6 or 8 selections of oysters. They are
pricy but succulent. Impressive cocktail menu.
Reservations recommended.

GUS'S WORLD-FAMOUS FRIED CHICKEN
310 S Front St Memphis, 901-527-4877
www.gusfriedchicken.com
CUISINE: Southern
DRINKS: Beer & Wine Only
SERVING: Lunch & Dinner

PRICE RANGE: $
NEIGHBORHOOD: Downtown
This place has been serving fried chicken for almost
60 years, not at this location, but the locals love it and
keep the place packed. There is a wait and it's one of
those old-school blues-infused Southern spots. The
menu offers fried chicken and a variety of sides, and
nothing else. Nothing. No frills here.

HOG & HOMINY
707 W Brookhaven Cir, Memphis, 901-207-7396
www.hogandhominy.com
CUISINE: Italian, Southern
DRINKS: Full Bar
SERVING: Lunch & Dinner daily
PRICE RANGE: $$
NEIGHBORHOOD: Brennan
This relaxed eatery situated in a renovated private
home has a bocce court on one side and a steel beer

tub bar out back that makes you feel like you might have stumbled into a frat party. But the food is dead serious, offering a unique mix of Italian and Southern cuisine. Where else can you get pork rinds made to order along with gnocchi? Somehow, it works. The simple menu features lots of product from local farmers. Buffalo-style pork tails; meatballs with guanciale, Parmesan; several pizzas—I liked the Red Eye best: pork belly, egg, Fontina, celery leaf. If you can handle it, the only dessert you should even think about is their peanut butter pie. Sickeningly good. The bar focuses on bourbons and creative cocktails. No reservations. This is the irreverent neighbor to **Andrew Michael Italian Kitchen** across the street at No. 712 that the owners of the H&H opened first, in 2008.

IRIS
2146 Monroe Ave, Memphis, 901-590-2828
www.restaurantiris.com
CUISINE: French; Cajun; Creole

DRINKS: Full bar
SERVING: Dinner nightly except Sunday, when its closed
PRICE RANGE: $$$
NEIGHBORHOOD: Midtown
The celebrated chef here is a guy named Kelly English, and his menu reflects his upbringing in southern Louisiana. He's become one of the most respected chefs in Memphis and won lots of awards. Iris is situated in a lovingly restored mid-century home. This place is located near historic Overton Square. Though the menu changes based on what's available locally different times of the year, expect items like: All spice seared duck breast; lobster "knuckle sandwich"; slow roasted lamb belly with charred corn; veal schnitzel with truffled mashed potatoes. Chef's menu also available, which is what I suggest you opt for. The chef has another restaurant right next door, a little less formal, called the **Second Line,** which is just as good in an entirely different way. Second Line is also a lot easier to get into than Iris. They share the same kitchen.

LAS TORTUGAS DELI MEXICANA
1215 S Germantown Rd, Germantown, 901-751-1200
www.delimexicana.com
CUISINE: Mexican
DRINKS: Beer & Wine Only
SERVING: Lunch & Dinner; closed Sun
PRICE RANGE: $$
NEIGHBORHOOD: Germantown
Casual café specializing in Mexican street food. Menu favorites include: De Carnitas Mexico City

made with barbecue pork and their Tacos. Bread baked fresh daily, which makes their Mexicans sandwiches so delectable. Fresh fruit juices are splendid and served with shaved ice. Worth the trip alone is the homemade guacamole, which explains why a lot of area chefs trek out here on their day off to eat such authentic food.

LAFAYETTE'S MUSIC ROOM
2119 Madison Ave, Memphis, 901-207-5097
www.lafayettes.com/memphis
CUISINE: American
DRINKS: Full Bar
SERVING: Lunch & Dinner
PRICE RANGE: $$
NEIGHBORHOOD: Midtown

Local restaurant/bar that serves Southern food with an attitude. Indoor—outdoor club features bands 7 nights a week. This is the place that helped launch the careers of such luminaries as Billy Joel, Big Star and KISS. Closed for many years, it reopened in 2014.

MOSA ASIAN BISTRO
850 S White Station, Memphis, 901-683-8889
www.mosaasianbistro.com
CUISINE: Asian Fusion / Korean BBQ
DRINKS: Beer & Wine Only
SERVING: Lunch & Dinner; Closed Mondays
PRICE RANGE: $$
NEIGHBORHOOD: Eastgate
Forget the unprepossessing storefront style exterior. Inside is a casual eatery offering delicious flavors and Korean BBQ. Favorites: Rainbow Panang Curry Chicken and Korean BBQ Beef. Asian bistro treats, curries, noodle dishes and spring rolls.

PAULETTE'S
River Inn
50 Harbor Town Sq, Memphis, 901-260-3300
www.paulettes.net
CUISINE: American (New)
DRINKS: Full Bar
SERVING: Breakfast, Lunch, & Dinner
PRICE RANGE: $$$
NEIGHBORHOOD: Mud Island

Out here on Mud Island (which has the Mississippi on the west and Wolf River Harbor on the east) is this cozy eatery that makes you feel like you're in a friend's house for a meal. Well, maybe your granny's house, because it is a little formal, but in a very comfortable Southern way, with the chairs looking like they came from someone's home, the antiques mixed in with the bric-a-brac on the walls, the china displays mounted above the doorways, all very nice. They offer a simple but interesting menu of American fare with French & Hungarian twists. Favorites: Filet Paulette and Red Wine Braised Short Ribs served with Gnocchi. Before or after dinner, check out the **Little Bar at Paulette's**. The mantelpiece came from an 1850s house in New Orleans. Cozy and friendly. Because they are part of the River Inn, they have to serve breakfast, which makes it a very nice place for you to take your morning meal if you're not staying at the River Inn. Right overlooking the water—hard to beat this place.

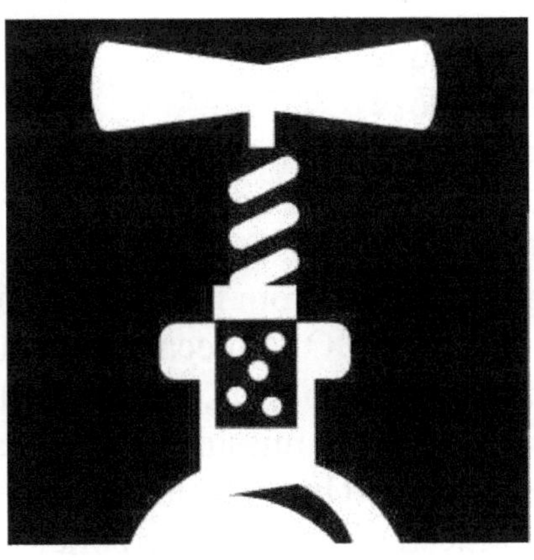

PAYNE'S ORIGINAL BAR-B-QUE

1762 Lamar Ave, Memphis, 901-272-1523
No web site
CUISINE: Barbeque
DRINKS: No Booze
SERVING: Lunch & Dinner
PRICE RANGE: $ - **cash only**
NEIGHBORHOOD: Med District

On your way into town from the airport is this place
that's been serving BBQ for decades in what used to
be an old gas station. No frills, but damned fine food.
Even the side dishes are missing here. It's all about
the BBQ. You have to bear in mind that in Memphis
BBQ doesn't mean ribs—it means pork shoulder.
Specifically, pork shoulder that's been pulled off the

bone and often chopped up and served with cole slaw on a bun. Sauce is either mild or hot. "One chopped hot" is what you want to order at Payne's. It's something in the slaw that goes with this pork sandwich that makes it so delicious. And if the chop is just right, you'll get a little crunchy crust mixed in with the moist meat. There's a unique sweetness to the sauce here that is unlike any other I've tasted in Memphis. Call up to make a to-go order and you'll hear the fine sound of chop-chop-chopping in the background. Cash only.

THE SECOND LINE

2144 Monroe Ave, Memphis, 901-590-2829
www.secondlinememphis.com
CUISINE: Cajun/Creole, Comfort Food
DRINKS: Full Bar
SERVING: Dinner nightly; lunch on weekends
PRICE RANGE: $$
NEIGHBORHOOD: Midtown
Located in a redesigned house from mid-century, this place is always busy and there's usually a wait. It's

not as fancy as its next door neighbor owned by the same chef, Chef Kelly English, <u>Iris</u>, which is much more formal than this place. Here the emphasis is on down home comfort food from southern Louisiana: Po'boys (several types: fried shrimp; braised chicken thighs & Swiss, which is my personal favorite; beef & gravy; catfish, BBQ shrimp); Andouille, crawfish & Pimento cheese Fries; seafood platters; fried oyster salad; crabmeat and corn hushpuppies. The heart-and-soul of Second Line is the bar, where the cocktails are handcrafted, each one made to order, including the fresh-squeezed juices. (There's a nice patio out back as well.) The food is just a fantastic add-on to what would be a great bar if it didn't have food.

SOUL FISH CAFÉ
4720 Poplar Ave, Memphis, 901-590-0323
<u>www.soulfishcafe.com</u>
CUISINE: Seafood

DRINKS: Beer & Wine Only
SERVING: Lunch & Dinner
PRICE RANGE: $$
NEIGHBORHOOD: Brennan
This seafood eatery offers great Southern dishes like
Fried Catfish and Po'boys made with Gambino bread
from New Orleans. Menu favorites include: Soul Fish
Platter and Smoked Pork chops. Popular family
dining destination with children's menu.

SWEET GRASS
937 Cooper St, Memphis, 901-278-0278
www.sweetgrassmemphis.com
CUISINE: Southern with some Italian
DRINKS: Full Bar
SERVING: Dinner nightly except Monday, when it's
closed; also brunch on Sunday
PRICE RANGE: $$
NEIGHBORHOOD: Cooper-Young

This small neighborhood bistro serves Low Country style cuisine with local ingredients, made by a chef who was a recent "Food & Wine" magazine best chef nominee. Chef Ryan Trimm's grandmother was Italian, and she taught him right. The place is a comfortable size with a bar that seats 8-10. The work of local artists is displayed on a rotating basis. If the weather's good, try for a seat on the patio outside. Menu favorites include: Braised Pork Cheeks; Mustard Glazed Grouper; osso bucco; housemade charcuterie platters with items like pork tongue paté, kielbasa, Cajun ham, liver loaf.

THREE LITTLE PIGS
5145 Quince Rd, Memphis, 901-685-7094
www.threelittlepigsbar-b-q.com
CUISINE: Barbeque
DRINKS: No
SERVING: Lunch & Dinner
PRICE RANGE:
NEIGHBORHOOD: Eastgate
A few minutes out of town is this cute little roadside BBQ spot is a locals' favorite serving Memphis-style pork shoulder barbeque. Great place for a quick lunch or to order food for the family to go. This is also a great stop for breakfast. Their motto is memorable: "We will Serve No Swine Before Its Time."

TOM'S BAR-B-Q & DELI

4087 New Getwell Rd, Memphis, 901-365-6690
www.tomsbarbeque.com
CUISINE: Barbeque
DRINKS: No Booze
SERVING: Lunch & Dinner, Closed Sunday
PRICE RANGE: $
NEIGHBORHOOD: Oakhaven
In business for over 30 years and is home to the
World Famous Rib Tips. (Rib tips are created when
ribs are cut St. Louis style. They're just leftovers. But
they are delicious, almost like chewy pieces of
crunchy leather, but oh, so good.) Menu includes
items like: Jumbo hot wings, BBQ chicken, pork
chops, and beef brisket. It's a dive but the food is
spectacular. Try the Channel Catfish Sandwich - it's a
winner

TOPS BAR-B-Q

6130 Macon Rd, Memphis, 901-371-0580
4183 Summer Ave, Memphis, 901-324-4325
2288 Frayser Blvd, Memphis, 901-353-4925
1286 Union Ave, Memphis, 901-725-7527
Among other locations…
https://topsbarbq.com/
CUISINE: Barbeque
DRINKS: No Booze
SERVING: Lunch & Dinner
PRICE RANGE: $
NEIGHBORHOOD: Barlett
Here's your simple fast food BBQ joint for those
needing a quick BBQ fix. This place celebrated their
60th anniversary in 2012 so they're doing something
right. Menu features variety of Bar-B-Q items like
ribs, brisket, and also offers great hamburgers.
Wherever you are in Memphis, you're likely close to
one of these places. (I've only listed 4 locations
above—there are a few more.) Their hickory-flavored

chopped BBQ sandwich topped with a coleslaw that's pungent with mustard is what you want to order.

TSUNAMI
928 Cooper St, Memphis, 901-274-2556
www.tsunamimemphis.com
CUISINE: Seafood/Tapas
DRINKS: Full Bar
SERVING: Dinner; closed Sun
PRICE RANGE: $$
NEIGHBORHOOD: Midtown
Popular eatery that offers a great menu of Pacific Rim small plates. Menu changes with the seasons.

YOUNG AVENUE DELI
2119 Young Ave, Memphis, 901-278-0034
www.youngavenuedeli.com
CUISINE: Deli
DRINKS: Full Bar

SERVING: Lunch & Dinner
PRICE RANGE: $
NEIGHBORHOOD: Cooper-Young
Basically a bar featuring live music but they do offer
a menu of lots of delicious salads and sandwiches.

Chapter 4
NIGHTLIFE

You've probably heard that Beale Street is the "Home of the Blues." And it is. You'll find an endless line of bars and lounges, a dizzying array of live music being offered in a lot of them. Pedestrians flock to the street at night and take it over, probably because they're allowed to drink as they stroll alone, picking up new drinks from each new place they pass. It's downright sinful.

Beale Street runs on for a bit, but the busiest portion is really quite small. You'll be surprised.

It had been the center of black life long ago, but hit a downturn that resulted in the whole street being abandoned, businesses boarded up and left to rot. It was reclaimed beginning in the 1980s when the city purchased a lot of the buildings and the revival began in spurts.

Now, millions of visitors come here to revel in the nightlife and music.

Beware Saturday night from 11 p.m. to 5 a.m. Sunday—this is the most dangerous time to be on Beale Street. The city still hasn't been able to curtail the violence.

CLUB RUMBA
303 S Main St, Memphis, 901-523-0020
www.memphisrumba.com
NEIGHBORHOOD: Downtown

A great place to slip into to dance with professional dancers if you don't have someone with you. Live band, salsa dancing, a bar. Small cover.

HAMMER & ALE
921 S Cooper, Memphis, 901-305-6930
www.hammerandale.com
NEIGHBORHOOD: Cooper-Young / Note: no cash; debit or credit cards only and they won't even run a tab. Go figure.
One of the best places in town known for its wide selection of craft beers on tap, including locally made brews.

KINGS PALACE CAFE'S ABSINTHE ROOM
162 Beale St, Memphis, 901-521-1851
www.kingspalacecafe.com
An intimate bar that specializes in absinthe. Follow the psychedelic staircase up to this unique bar that features 3 pool rooms, 2 overlooking Beale Street.

MOLLIE FONTAINE LOUNGE

679 Adams Ave, Memphis, 901-524-1886
www.molliefontainelounge.com
NEIGHBORHOOD: Downtown
Has a little bit of everything going on here, from the
serene piano bar downstairs where someone will be
playing and singing to an upstairs room which is
more lounge-like to a clubby scene with a DJ to a
restaurant serving very nice food. All located in an
old Victorian manse once inhabited by the
eponymous Mollie Fontaine.

RUM BOOGIE CAFÉ

182 Beale St, Memphis, 91-528-0150
http://rumboogie.com
NEIGHBORHOOD: Downtown
Their motto here is, "Eat, Drink, Boogie, Repeat."
And that pretty much sums it up. Come for the music,
the great selection of rums and beer, since you're
down here on Beale Street, but skip the BBQ. There

are too many other great BBQ places in Memphis to
eat it here.

PAULA AND RAIFORD'S DISCO
14 S 2nd St, Memphis, 901-521-2494
http://paularaifords.com/home.html
NEIGHBORHOOD: Downtown
Great dancing in this 2-level club with great music,
relaxing couches, a fog machine, busy DJs.

SILLY GOOSE

100 Peabody Pl, Memphis, 901-435-6915
www.sillygoosememphis.com
NEIGHBORHOOD: Downtown
A good option for dancing to DJs and craft cocktails in this hip and trendy lounge. Has a modest menu of snacks and a couple of sandwiches (burgers, pulled pork), pizzas.

WILD BILL'S

1580 Vollintine Ave, Memphis, 901-206-3272
www.wildbillsmemphis.com
NEIGHBORHOOD: Vollintine
This club is legendary for the live blues acts and has
hosted everyone from B.B. King to Buddy Guy. One
good way to save on wall treatments and décor? Let
everybody and his cousin tack up their own pictures,
like prisoners who want to leave a memorial that they
were here. They only serve beer, big beers, the 40-
ounce size. They also have a great house band, an
open kitchen, a friendly bar, and a small dance floor.
Modest cover charge. Cash only.

Chapter 5
WHAT TO SEE & DO

AUTOZONE PARK
200 Union Ave, Downtown Memphis, 901-721-6000
https://www.milb.com/memphis
The Cardinals Triple-A affiliate plays in this lovely
park located in the heart of Downtown Memphis,
AutoZone Park was named the 2009 Minor League
Ballpark of the Year by *Baseball America*. By
combining the feel of such parks as Wrigley Field,
Fenway Park, and Camden Yards, AutoZone Park is a
state-of-the-art facility with classic, neo-traditional
style.

BACKBEAT TOURS
BB KING'S BLUE'S CLUB
197 Beale St, Memphis, 901-527-9415

This company offers a variety of tour from the highly rated Memphis Mojo Tour (a combination of live music, comedy, an narration that takes you through Memphis' musical heritage) to the popular Graceland Tour. Other tours available: Memphis Discovery Tour, Historic Memphis Walking Tour, and the Memphis Ghost Tour. Tours are a step-on service but private tours are available. Rates vary depending on tour.

FULL GOSPEL TABERNACLE CHURCH

787 Hale Road, Memphis, 901-345-8040
NEIGHBORHOOD: Whitehaven
Started by Al Green in 1979, this is a popular church for visitors who often take up half the pews. Here you'll hear some exciting gospel but the main attraction is the Reverend Al Green. Services are at 11:15. Dress properly if you go.

GRACELAND

3734 Elvis Presley Blvd, Memphis, 901-332-3322
<u>www.graceland.com</u>
NEIGHBORHOOD: Whitehaven
Home of Elvis Presley, "The King of Rock and Roll." It's no surprise that this is the No. 1 tourist attraction in Memphis. (It's the second most visited private residence in the USA, topped only by something called the White House.)

Think "tacky tourist" trap but don't miss it—you might be pleasantly surprised. Although it is not advisable to venture in the suburbs surrounding the site, there are lots and lots of Elvis-related stuff to see here—the house itself (note that the upper floor, with Elvis's bedroom and Lisa Marie's nursery, is not open to the public), customized private airplanes, an automobile collection, gold records, costumes, the check Elvis wrote as a down payment, architectural drawings, and more.

Elvis was not the big star he later became when he bought Graceland. A newspaper publisher named S.E. Toof owned the 13-acre spread and named it for his daughter, Grace. Elvis took over in 1957, paying $102,000 for it. He added an indoor waterfall, furniture upholstered with what looks like fur, a pool, and other modifications to make it as tacky as he could. (He succeeded.)

He's buried outside next to his parents.

Take note of Elvis Week ("Death Week" to the locals) in early August, culminating in the candlelight

vigil on the anniversary of Elvis's death. It is
a big deal, which can be a good thing or a bad thing,
depending on your perspective.

Check out the bizarre felt-pen scribblings on the
fence, some hip-ironic, some of the psycho-lunatic-
fan sort.

If you happen to be in Memphis during Birth or
Death Week - January and August, respectively - sit
downtown for a few hours just to watch the Elvis
fans. This is the only town besides Vegas where you
see people dressed like Elvis not just on Halloween,
but every day.

JERRY'S SNO CONES
1657 Wells Station Rd, Memphis, 901-767-2659
www.jerryssnowcones.com
This place has every snow cone known to man or so it
seems. Also served is soft-serve ice cream and
delicious pesto burgers.

MEMPHIS BOTANIC GARDEN
750 Cherry Rd, Memphis, 901-636-4100

<u>www.memphisbotanicgarden.com</u>
NEIGHBORHOOD: Audubon-Oak Court
With over 96 acres of natural woodlands and cultivated gardens, the garden is also home to the outdoor concert series 'Live at the Garden' and the renowned Japanese Garden of Tranquility. A recent addition is "My Big Backyard." a 2.5-acre children's garden with a larger-than-life birdhouse, a tunneling adventure, a teaching pond, "leaping lawn," "critter creek," and many other spaces that cater to children of all ages.

MEMPHIS ROCK 'N SOUL MUSEUM
191 Beale St, Memphis, 901-205-2533
<u>www.memphisrocknsoul.com</u>
NEIGHBORHOOD: Downtown
This museum offers visitors a glimpse at the Memphis music scene from the rural music of the 1930s to the heyday in the '70s and including its global musical influence. The museum's digital audio

tour guide includes over 300 minutes of info and over 100 songs. The museum exhibits a variety of musical instruments, costumes, and treasures in seven galleries. A must-see is the exhibition about the birth of rock and soul music that was created by the Smithsonian Institution. You can learn how the white wrestler Suptnik Monroe used his black fan base as leverage to integrate the Memphis city auditorium back in the 1950s. Museum and gift shop open 10 a.m. to 7 p.m. daily. Admission fee.

MEMPHIS ZOO

2000 Prentiss Place, Memphis, 901-333-6500
www.memphiszoo.org
NEIGHBORHOOD: Midtown
Set on 76 acres, this zoo is home to over 3,500 animals with over 500 different species represented. The zoo features three zones with 19 exhibits including: Teton Trek, Northwest Passage and China, and is home to the giant Pandas Ya Ya and Le Le.

The zoo features many annual events like the Zoo Brews beer tasting from around the world. Open daily 9 a.m. to 5 p.m. (4 p.m. in the winter). Admission fee.

NATIONAL CIVIL RIGHTS MUSEUM
450 Mulberry St, Memphis, 901-521-9699
www.civilrightsmuseum.org
NEIGHBORHOOD: Downtown
This privately-owned complex of museums and historic buildings celebrates the history of the Civil Rights Movement. The museum is built around the site where Martin Luther King, Jr., was assassinated on April 4, 1968. Two other buildings also connected with the King assassination are included in the complex. They have a replica of a slave ship that you can go into to feel what it was like to be squeezed shoulder to shoulder with other slaves. A mock courtroom is there for you to experience the famous Brown v. Board of Education Supreme Court decision. Another exhibit offers music and poetry from the Black Power Movement of the 1960s and 1970s. There's even a replica of the bus Rosa Parks rode the day she refused to go to the back of the bus in Montgomery. The museum collection includes 260 artifacts, over 40 films, and oral histories. Visitors can experience the museum via external listening posts that take you through five centuries of history. Open daily, closed Tuesday. Nominal admission fee.

THE ORPHEUM THEATRE MEMPHIS
203 S Main St, Memphis, 901-525-3000
https://orpheum-memphis.com/
NEIGHBORHOOD: Downtown
This grand, gilded historic 1928 theater is one of the
few remaining movie palaces of the 1920s, with some
2,400 seats. Now the theater hosts traveling
Broadway shows during the year and features a movie
series in the summer. Tours are open to the public
several times during the year. (This is much more
interesting than I'm making it out to be, so really try
to make time for this tour.)

OVERTON PARK
1914 Poplar Ave, Memphis, 901-214-5450
www.overtonpark.org
A 342-acre public park that features a nine-hole golf
course, the Memphis Brooks Museum of Art, the
Memphis Zoo, the Memphis College of Art, the

Levitt Shell, Rainbow Lake, two playgrounds, and the 126-acre Old Forest State Natural Area.

PINK PALACE MUSEUM & PLANETARIUM
3050 Central Ave, Memphis, 901-636-2362
www.memphismuseums.org
NEIGHBORHOOD: Chickasaw Gardens
Built as a private residence by Clarence Saunders, the man who introduced Piggly Wiggly, the mansion has now been transformed into a major science and historical museum. Here you'll find exhibits ranging from archeology to chemistry displaying everything from shrunken heads to animatronic dinosaurs. The Planetarium features a 165-seat theater-in-the-round auditorium and projects star fields, images, and laser

images on the domed ceiling. The venue also includes
an IMAX Theater, which opened in 1995 with a four-
story movable screen. Open daily. Admisson fee
determined by number of venues visited.

REDBIRDS

198 Union Ave, Memphis, 901-721-6000
www.memphisredbirds.com
NEIGHBORHOOD: Downtown
The Cardinals Triple-A affiliate plays at a snazzy
downtown stadium, complete with the sort of contests
and fans-on-field participation you get when you
cross corporate America and minor league baseball.
(The Burger King-sponsors a race where contestants
dress as hamburger buns and make a human burger.)
The home games are played at AutoZone Park in

downtown Memphis. The club offers several community programs and operates the Memphis Redbirds Foundations that funds a program that enables local children to participate in sports.

MEEMAN-SHELBY FOREST STATE PARK
910 Riddick Rd, Millington, 901-876-5215
www.tnstateparks.com/parks/about/meeman-shelby
This natural state park features 14,475 acres of hardwood bottomland that borders the Mississippi River. The park offers over 20 miles of hiking trails that are open for horses and hikers. Camping opportunities abound throughout the park and there are six two-bedroom vacation cabins available located on the shore of Poplar Tree Lake. There are 49 campsites throughout the park, all equipped with table, grill, electrical and water hookups. The park features mature Bald Cypress, Tupelo swamp, and the majestic Chickasaw Bluffs. The park features many endangered and protected plants and wild animals like deer, turkey, otter, beaver, foxes, and bobcat. There are over 200 species of songbirds, waterfowl, shorebirds, and birds of prey, including the American Bald Eagle living in the park. The Nature Center is open Fri – Sun from 10 a.m. to 5 p.m. and closed an hour at lunchtime. Here you'll find exhibits of live snakes, salamanders, turtles, fish aquariums, and an indoor live butterfly garden. The park is also home to a 36-hole disc golf course that is divided into two 18-hole courses.

STAX MUSEUM OF AMERICAN SOUL MUSIC

926 E McLemore Ave, Memphis, 888-942-7685
www.staxmuseum.com
NEIGHBORHOOD: Southside
Housed in the former **Capitol Theatre**, this is a
replica of the Stax recording studio and a museum
dedicated to soul music. The museum features more
than 2,000 videos, films, photographs, original
instruments, stage costumes, memorabilia and
interactive exhibits. This is the same site of Stax
Records where Isaac Hayes, the Staple Singers,
Albert King, Otis Redding and the Bay-Kays, among
many others, recorded their music from the 1950s till
the company went bankrupt in the 1970s. Exhibits
include: the Soul Train dance floor and Hayes's
restored 1972 gold-trimmed peacock-blue Cadillac El
Dorado. The building also houses The Soulsville
Charter School. Nominal admission fee. Open Tues –
Sun, closed Mon. The gift shop is worth a little extra
time.

TOPS GALLERY

400 South Front, Memphis, 901-340-0134
www.topsgallery.com
NEIGHBORHOOD: Downtown
This old industrial building has been converted into a
showcase for contemporary art. Down in the
basement in what used to be a room used for storing
coal you'll find exhibits featuring work of artists such
as Chris Dorland, Corinne Jones, Sarah Jones, Seth
Kelly, Lester Merriweather, Terri Phillips, Walter
Robinson, Victoria Sambunaris, Igor Siddiqui, and
Dan Torop. Open Saturdays: 1 – 6 p.m. or by
appointment.

Chapter 6
SHOPPING & SERVICES

BASS PRO SHOPS AT THE PYRAMID
1 Bass Pro Dr, Memphis, 901-291-8200
www.basspro.com
NEIGHBORHOOD: Uptown
When you see the pyramid, you'll think you're in Las Vegas. This wilderness-themed retail space gives the feeling of entering a real-life swamp filled with fish and gators. Everything Bass Pro is here from shirts to guns. There's also a small man-made river filled with fish. You can climb the stairs of the deck for free but for a small fee you can take the elevator – and it's worth the ride.

BURKE'S BOOK STORE
936 Cooper St, Memphis, 901-278-7484
www.burkesbooks.com/
Cozy, neighborhood bookstore that features a large
selection of Memphis authors and books about
Memphis. They also have shelves of cheap
paperbacks and a table of free books (free after you
spend $10).

CROSSTOWN ARTS
1350 Concourse Ave, Memphis, 901-507-8030
www.crosstownarts.org
NEIGHBORHOOD: Crosstown; Med District
This is a performance and exhibition venue that
promotes a variety of mediums including exhibition,
performance, production, education, and retail. The
space is open for artists and performers to host arts-

related events. You might find a bluegrass band playing one week and an all-drag dance show the next.

GINO PAMBIANCHI

https://rawartists.com/ginopambianchi
Pambianchi is a Memphis-based illustrator, screen printer and designer. Visit his website or contact him to drop in at his workspace where you can find him drawing.

GONER RECORDS

2152 Young Ave, Memphis, 901-722-0095
www.goner-records.com
This record shop is legendary and features a large variety of bands and artist under the Goner Records label.

JARED SMALL

4540 Poplar Ave, Memphis, 901-767-3800
www.jaredsmall.com/
Jared Small is a local painter who paints scenes of the South. His work has been described as "imagining other people's memories." Contact him to visit his home studio.

ME & MRS JONES

600 S Perkins Rd, Memphis, 901-494-8786
www.mrsjonespaintedfinishes.com
A craft boutique that offers classes in everything from painting furniture to stenciling and upholstery. Interesting selection of painted furniture.

THE OTHERLANDS COFFEE BAR

641 S Cooper St, Memphis, 901-278-4994
http://otherlandscoffeebar.com/
NEIGHBORHOOD: Midtown
The funky little coffee bar is also a gift shop. It's also
a great place to relax and hear some good live music.
The bar offers coffee, organic teas and homemade
soups. The gift shop showcases the works of local
artists. Free Wi-Fi.

PALLADIO ANTIQUES & ART

2169 Central Ave, Memphis, 901-276-3808
www.palladioantiques.com
One of the best antique shops in Memphis. A great
selection of unique furniture, accessories, art, and
rugs. Stop by to shop and have lunch in the café.

PAPER & CLAY

525 S Main St, Memphis, 901-347-3766
www.shoppaperandclay.com
This is a small ceramics studio that showcases the modern and yet very functional and reasonably priced pieces by artist Brit McDaniel. Studio visits by appointment. (Well worth a call to stop by—you'll buy something, I promise you, like her coffee mugs below—I just love the handle.)

SHELBY FOREST GENERAL STORE
7729 Benjestown Rd, Millington, 901-876-5770
www.shelbyforestgeneralstore.com
NEIGHBORHOOD: Millington
This store stocks everything that you might need from
dry goods, live bait, cold drinks, Frisbees, and food
prepared fresh from the grill. You can even get your
fishing and hunting licenses here, as this is also a
game-check station. Conveniently located between
the front and rear entrances to Meeman-Shelby State
Park.

SHELBY FOREST TAXIDERMY

5586 Benjestown Rd, Memphis, 901-493-8370
www.shelbyforesttaxidermy.com
NEIGHBORHOOD: Millington
This is your one-stop taxidermy shop as they do everything including birds, fish, and mammals. Their motto is "the taxidermy shop that recreates your hunting and fishing memories."

<u>INDEX</u>

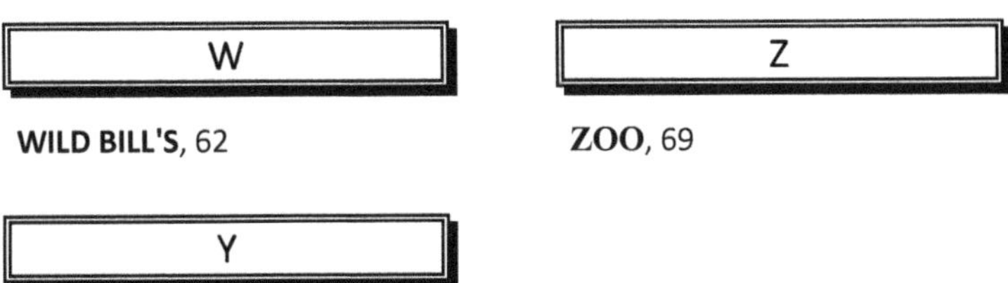

WILD BILL'S, 62

ZOO, 69

YOUNG AVENUE DELI, 53